ICONS

PROVENCE STYLE

PROVENC

Landscapes Houses

Interiors Details

E STYLE

TASCHEN

KÖLN LONDON LOS ANGELES MADRID PARIS TOKYO

COVER: A garden high in the Lubéron – the mountain region of Provence.
COUVERTURE: *Jardin, dans les hauteurs du Lubéron – paysage provençal de montagne.*
UMSCHLAGVORDERSEITE: Garten hoch oben im Lubéron – einer Berglandschaft der Provence.

Photo: Guy Hervais

Also available from TASCHEN:

- **Provence Interiors**
Trilingual edition, 300 pages
3–8228–8176–7
3–8228–8340–9 (French cover)

© 2002 TASCHEN GmbH
Hohenzollernring 53, D-50672 Köln
www.taschen.com

Edited by Angelika Taschen, Cologne
Cover design by Angelika Taschen, Claudia Frey, Cologne
Texts edited by Stephanie Bischoff, Cologne
Lithography by Horst Neuzner, Cologne
English translation: Deborah Foulkes, Cologne
French translation: Anne Charrière, Croissy Seine
Printed in Italy
ISBN 3–8228–1639–6

CONTENTS SOMMAIRE INHALT

Ah, Provence: that immortal region, the indefatigable destination of charm-hungry tourists and old world purists. Resting snugly in France's southeastern corner, Provence is world-renowned not only for its breathtaking landscapes, but also for its cultural richness – a mélange of Mediterranean influences – and delightful cuisine. The essence of a true Provençal home lies in its unpretentious simplicity. Those with ancestral roots in the region shrug off notions of décor and style, though their houses – complete with coarse stone walls, terracotta tile floors (tomettes), and inimitable smoke-tainted hearths – seem to have effortless charm and are the envy of home decoration magazine readers world-wide; others who have chosen to transplant themselves in Provence, or to take on vacation cottages there, strive to obtain Provençal legitimacy through more purposeful means

LAVENDER FIELDS FOREVER
Alison Castle

Ah! Provence! Région immortelle, destination inlassable des touristes assoiffés de tes charmes et des amoureux inconditionnels de vestiges anciens. Confortablement lovée au sud-est de la France, la Provence est mondialement connue, non seulement pour ses paysages exceptionnels, mais aussi pour sa richesse culturelle – mélange d'influences méditerranéennes – et sa merveilleuse cuisine. La quintessence d'une véritable maison provençale réside dans sa simplicité. Pour ceux qui ont leurs racines en Provence depuis des générations, des mots comme « ornement » ou « style » n'ont pas d'usage, bien que leurs maisons – avec leurs murs de pierres grossièrement taillées, leurs sols dallés de tomettes et leurs inimitables cheminées aux teintes fumées – semblent exhaler un charme irrésistible, faisant pâlir d'envie les lecteurs de magazines d'architecture et d'aménagement intérieur du monde entier ; d'autres, qui ont choisi de s'installer en Provence ou y ont acheté une maison de vacances, essaient à leur

Ahh, die Provence, diese unsterbliche Region, Ziel unermüdlicher, charme-hungriger Touristen. In bevorzugter Lage im Südosten Frankreichs gelegen, ist die Provence weltweit berühmt für ihre atemberaubenden Landschaften, für ihren kulturellen Reichtum – eine Melange zahlreicher mediterraner Einflüsse –, und für ihre köstliche Küche. Die Essenz eines typisch provenzalischen Hauses liegt in seiner unprätentiösen Schlichtheit, und für diejenigen, die in der Region seit Generationen verwurzelt sind, klingen »Dekor« und »Stil« wie Fremdwörter, denn ihre Häuser – aus groben Steinmauern, mit Terrakottafliesen (Tomettes genannt) und den unnachahmlichen, rußgeschwärzten Kaminen – haben einen völlig ungezwungenen, selbstverständlichen Charme und erregen damit die neidvolle Bewunderung derjenigen, die Architektur- und Interieur-Zeitschriften lesen. Und die, die sich erst vor kurzem in der Provence niedergelassen haben oder dort nur ein Ferienhaus besitzen, streben stilbewusst und ent-

(sometimes with the help of such aforementioned periodicals or, perhaps, with books such as the present volume). Herein you'll traverse a wordless cross-section of Provence images, each as lovely as one would imagine in one's dreams, together painting a vivid mosaic of Provençal living. Imagine yourself in one of these gardens, having a lazy afternoon siesta under the cool shadow of an oak tree, lulled by the music of crickets. From fields of lavender (whose scent practically emanates from the page) to sculpted terrace gardens and homey kitchens, these scenes represent the quintessential Provence that is as perfect in reality as in the most fanciful of imaginations. It is no wonder that Cézanne and Van Gogh were inspired so intensely by Provence's picturesque panorama.

façon d'acquérir la citoyenneté provençale, en s'aidant des revues déjà citées ou de livres comme celui-ci. Dans les pages qui suivent, vous êtes invités à une promenade sans parole à travers un choix d'images de Provence, toutes aussi belles que dans vos rêves. Ensemble, elles forment une mosaïque vivante de la vie provençale. Imaginez-vous dans l'un de ces jardins, en train de faire la sieste à l'ombre fraîche d'un chêne, bercés par le chant des grillons. Ou découvrez des champs de lavande (on croit presque en sentir le parfum) et de subtils jardins en terrasses. Pénétrez plus avant, jusque dans l'intimité des cuisines. Vous percevez alors l'essence de la Provence, aussi parfaite dans la réalité que dans vos imaginations les plus vives. Et vous comprenez par quel mystère Cézanne et Van Gogh se sont laissé si puissamment inspirer par les pittoresques paysages de Provence.

schlossen danach, sich ihrer Wahlheimat anzugleichen (und manchmal suchen sie hierbei Anregungen in den erwähnten Zeitschriften oder in Büchern wie diesem). Auf den folgenden Seiten blättern Sie durch einen wortlosen Querschnitt von Bildern der Provence, jedes so wunderschön wie man sie sich im Traum vorstellt, und alle zusammen fügen sich zu einem lebendigen Mosaik des provenzalischen Lebensstils. Stellen Sie sich vor, Sie befinden sich in einem der Gärten und verbringen Ihre Siesta im kühlen Schatten einer Eiche, sanft eingelullt vom Zirpen der Grillen. Von den Lavendelfeldern (deren Duft förmlich aus diesen Buchseiten strömt), bis zu den kunstvoll gestalteten Terrassengärten und den gemütlichen Küchen, all diese Eindrücke sind der Inbegriff der Provence, bei der sich die Wirklichkeit mit den schönsten Fantasien trifft. Kein Wunder, dass Cézanne und Van Gogh von den pittoresken Panoramen der Provence so inspiriert wurden.

"Provence has a thousand faces, a thousand aspects, a thousand characters, and it is wrong to describe it as a single and indivisble phenomenon."

Jean Giono

«La Provence présente mille visages, mille facettes, mille personnalités et il est vain de la décrire comme un phénomène unique et indivisible.»

Jean Giono

»Die Provence hat tausend Gesichter, tausend Aspekte, tausend Charaktere, und es ist falsch, sie als ein einziges, unteilbares Phänomen darzustellen.«

Jean Giono

GARDENS & TERRACES

Jardins & Terrasses Gärten & Terrassen

10/11 Lavender fields, consisting of a total of 1700 plants. *Champs de lavande, comptant au total 1700 plants.* Lavendelfelder, die aus insgesamt 1.700 Pflanzen angelegt sind. Bruno, Dominique and Alexandre Lafourcade, Provence. Photo: Deidi von Schaewen

12/13 A garden high in the Lubéron – the mountain region of Provence. *Jardin, dans les hauteurs du Lubéron – paysage provençal de montagne.* Garten hoch oben im Lubéron – einer Berglandschaft der Provence. Photo: Guy Hervais

14/15 Garden of a former farmhouse. *Jardin d'une ancienne ferme.* Garten eines ehemaligen Bauernhauses. Hôtel La Bastide de Marie, Ménerbes Photo: Guy Hervais/ Philippe Seuilliet

16/17 Fabulous swimming pool in Provençal surroundings. *Piscine de rêve dans un décor provençal.* Traumhaftes Schwimmbad in provenzialischer Umgebung. Hôtel La Bastide de Marie, Ménerbes Photo: Guy Hervais/ Philippe Seuilliet

18/19 Table laid for refreshments in picturesque French landscape. *Table mise dans un paysage pittoresque.* Gedeckter Tisch in malerischer französischer Landschaft. Hôtel La Bastide de Marie, Ménerbes Photo: Guy Hervais/ Philippe Seuilliet

20/21 Hundred-year-old house in a beautiful area of France. *Maison séculaire dans une belle région de France.* Jahrhunderte altes Haus in einer wunderschönen Region Frankreichs. La Villa St. Louis, Lourmarin Photo: Guy Hervais

22/23 Veranda with wrought-iron chairs and a thatched roof. *Terrasse avec chaises en fer forgé sous un toit de chaume.* Terrasse mit schmiedeeisernen Stühlen und einem Strohdach. Hôtel La Bastide de Marie, Ménerbes Photo: Guy Hervais/ Philippe Seuilliet

24/25 Bistro table and garden chairs invite one to take an aperitif. *Tables bistrot et chaises de jardin invitent à l'apéritif.* Bistrotische und Gartenstühle laden zu einem Apéritiv ein. Photo: Mirjam Bleeker/Taverne Agency; Styling: Je Krings

26/27 This place is a dream for sunbathing. *Cet endroit rêvé pour un bain de soleil.* Ein traumhafter Platz für ein Bad in der Sonne. Photo: Mirjam Bleeker/Taverne Agency; Styling: Je Krings

28/29 Table laid for dinner on the veranda of a house. *Table dressé sur la terrasse d'une maison.* Gedeckter Tisch auf der Terrasse eines Hauses. Photo: Mirjam Bleeker/Taverne Agency; Styling: Je Krings

30/31 17th century summer-house of Lillian Williams. *Ancienne maison de plaisance du 17ᵉ siècle de Lillian Williams.* Altes Lusthaus aus dem 17.Jh. von Lillian Williams. Photo: Deidi von Schaewen/ Philippe Seuilliet

32/33 The Château de Castellaras on a hill north of Cannes. *Le Château de Castellaras, sur une colline au nord de Cannes.* Das Château de Castellaras auf einem Hügel nördlich von Cannes. Photo: Deidi von Schaewen/ Philippe Seuilliet

34/35 The old arches of the Castellaras lend the inner courtyard its charm. *Ces arcades anciennes de Castellaras font le charme de la cour intérieure.* Die alten Rundbögen des Castellaras machen den Charme des Innenhofes aus.
Photo: Deidi von Schaewen/ Philippe Seuilliet

36/37 Little house surrounded by nature of Mont Ventoux. *Maisonnette au milieu d'une nature en fleur a mont Ventoux.* Kleines Häuschen, umgeben von der blühenden Natur des Mont Ventoux.
Photo: Guy Hervais

38/39 The dog enjoys a run in the magnificent landscape of Lubéron. *Le chien se réjouit de gambader dans le magnifique pay-sage du Lubéron.* Der Hund genießt den Auslauf in der großartigen Landschaft des Lubéron.
Photo: Guy Hervais

40/41 Romantic seating with a view near Vaison-la-Romaine. *Point de vue romantique près de Vaison-la-Romaine.* Romantischer Sitzplatz mit Aussicht in der Nähe von Vaison-la- Romaine.
Photo: Guy Hervais

42/43 A seating arrangement among the designed flowerbeds of Nicole de Vésian. *Sièges entre les plates-bandes de Nicole de Vésian.* Ein Sitzplatz zwischen den von Nicole de Vésian angelegten Beeten.
Photo: Deidi von Schaewen/ Philippe Seuilliet

44/45 Small channel is framed by large terracotta pots with olive trees. *Petit canal bordé d'oliviers poussant dans de grands pots en terre cuite.* Ein kleiner Kanal wird von Olivenbäumen in Terrakottagefäßen eingerahmt.
Photo: Deidi von Schaewen

46/47 Steps connect the terraces of the garden. *Un escalier relie les terrasses du jardin.* Eine Treppe verbindet die verschiedenen Terrassen des Gartens miteinander.
Photo: Deidi von Schaewen/ Philippe Seuilliet

48/49 A terrace at the pond, surrounded by Mediterranean plants. *Au bord d'un bassin, une terrasse entour de plantes méditerranéennes.* Eine Terrasse am Wasserbecken, umgeben von mediterranen Pflanzen.
Photo: Deidi von Schaewen

"…Mistral's bedroom… a modest peasant's room, with two large beds. The walls had no paper on them, on the ceiling the rafters remained exposed…"

Alphonse Daudet: The Poet Mistral, in: Letters from my Windmill

«…la chambre de Mistral… une modeste chambre de paysan, avec deux grands lits. Les murs n'ont pas de papier; les solives du plafond se voient…»

Alphonse Daudet, Le Poète Mistral, dans *Lettres de mon moulin*

»…Mistrals Zimmer… eine bescheidene Bauernstube mit zwei grossen Betten. Die Wänden sind nicht tapeziert, die Deckenbalken offen zu sehen…«

Alphonse Daudet, Der Dichter Mistral, in: *Briefe aus meiner Mühle*

HOUSES & INTERIORS

Maisons & Intérieurs Häuser & Interieurs

54/55 Dining room with typical Provençal chairs. *Salle à manger avec chaises typiquement provençales.* Esszimmer mit typisch provenzialischen Stühlen.
Photo: Maison Française/Françoise Lemarchand/Inside

56/57 A bedroom with folding tables as bedside tables. *La chambre à coucher avec ses tables de nuit pliantes.* Ein Schlafzimmer mit Klapptischen als Nachttisch.
Photo: Maison Française/Françoise Lemarchand/Inside

58/59 View of a comfortable kitchen with rustic wooden table. *Vue d'une cuisine fonctionnelle avec table en bois rustique.* Ansicht einer funktionellen Küche mit rustikalem Holztisch.
Photo: Maison Française/Françoise Lemarchand/Inside

60/61 A view of the Façade of a Provençal house. *Vue sur la Façade de la maison provençale.* Ein Blick auf die Fassade eines provenzialischen Hauses.
Photo: Deidi von Schaewen

62/63 Salon furnished with antique pieces and a old chandelier. *Salon avec des meubles anciens et un vieux lustre.* Salon mit antiken Möbeln und altem Leuchter eingerichtet.
Photo: Deidi von Schaewen

64/65 French traditionally furnished and decorated bedroom. *Chambre à coucher meublée et décorée dans le style traditionnel français.* Französich traditionell eingerichtetes und dekoriertes Schlafzimmer.
Photo: Deidi von Schaewen

66/67 Garden view of the tower room of the Castellaras. *Jardin de Castellaras : vue sur la chambre de la tour.* Blick vom Garten auf das Turmzimmer des Castellaras.
Photo: Deidi von Schaewen/ Philippe Seuilliet

68/69 Lounge with open hearth, furnished with a few antique pieces. *Chambre avec cheminée, aménagée sobrement, avec quelques meubles anciens.* Mit wenigen antiken Möbeln eingerichtetes Kaminzimmer.
Photo: Deidi von Schaewen/Philippe Seuilliet

70/71 Heavy antique table in the renovated stables. *La vieeille table en bois massive dans une ancienne écurie.* Antiker, schwerer Holztisch in dem ehemaligen Pferdestall.
Photo: Deidi von Schaewen/ Philippe Seuilliet

72/73 Bedroom with an old wooden four-poster bed. *Chambre à coucher avec ancien lit à baldaquin en bois.* Schlafzimmer mit einem alten Himmelbett aus Holz.
Photo: Deidi von Schaewen/ Philippe Seuilliet

74/75 Antique, hand-painted window shutters cut out the harsh sunlight. *Des volets anciens, peints à la main, tamisent la lumière aveuglante du soleil.* Antike, handbemalte Fensterläden dämpfen das grelle Sonnenlicht.
Photo: Deidi von Schaewen/Philippe Seuilliet

76/77 Cosy bedroom with large chequered wall decor. *Chambre à coucher harmonieuse, aver décoration murale à grands carreaux.* Gemütliches Schlafzimmer mit großflächig karierter Wanddekoration.
Photo: Deidi von Schaewen/Philippe Seuilliet

78/79 Dining room with silver baroque candle-holders on the table. *Salle à manger avec chandeliers baroques en argent sur la table.* Esszimmer mit barocken Silberleuchtern auf dem Tisch.
Mervé Thibault, France
Photo: Deidi von Schaewen

80/81 Open-ended room with traditional library. *Pièce de passage avec bibliothèque traditionnelle.* Durchgangszimmer mit traditioneller Bibliothek.
Mervé Thibault, France
Photo: Deidi von Schaewen

82/83 A cosy winter kitchen with a gaming table as dining table. *Petite cuisine d'hiver avec table de jeu servant aux repas.* Gemütliche Winterküche mit Spieltisch als Esstisch.
Mervé Thibault, France
Photo: Deidi von Schaewen

84/85 Changing corner in the bathroom with old cupboard doors. *Coin de la salle de bains, avec portes d'armoires anciennes.* Ankleide-ecke im Badezimmer mit alten Schranktüren.
Mervé Thibault, France
Photo: Deidi von Schaewen

86/87 Guest room with a Louis XVI four-poster bed. *Chambre avec lit à baldaquin Louis XVI.* Gästezimmer mit Himmelbett aus der Epoche Ludwig XVI.
Mervé Thibault, France
Photo: Deidi von Schaewen

88/89 Sunshine yellow bedroom with old furniture. *Chambre à coucher jaune soleil avec mobilier ancien.* Sonnengelbes Schlafzimmer mit alten Möbeln.
Mervé Thibault, France
Photo: Deidi von Schaewen

90/91 A fancy old chandelier gives the room a decorative touch. *Pièce ornée d'un vieux lustre en à volutes orné de bougies.* Ein alter verschnörkelter Kerzenleuchter ziert den Raum.
Les Arnajons, Le Puy Sainte Reparade
Photo: Philippe Saharoff/Inside

92/93 Laid table with large open hearth in the background. *Table dressée devant la grande cheminée.* Gedeckter Tisch mit großem offenem Kamin im Hintergrund.
Les Arnajons, Le Puy Sainte Reparade
Photo: Philippe Saharoff/Inside

94/95 Canary yellow kitchen with a fireplace dating from 1760. *Cuisine jaune canari avec cheminée datant de 1760.* Kanariengelbe Küche mit einem Kamin aus dem Jahr 1760.
Photo: Guillaume de Laubier/Maison Française
Inside

96/97 The former hayloft is now the bedroom. *Grenier transformé en chambre à coucher.* Der ehemalige Heuboden ist heute das Schlafzimmer.
Photo: Guillaume de Laubier/Maison Française
Inside

98/99 The walls of the bedroom have been plastered with lavender tones. *Les murs de la chambre à coucher sont crépi de tons lavande.* Die Wände im Schlafzimmer sind in Lavendeltönen gehalten.
Photo: Guillaume de Laubier/Maison Française
Inside

100/101 The bedrooms walls are covered with white rough wood planking. *Chambre à coucher blanche, murs lambrissés de lattes de bois grossières.* Die Schlafzimmerwände sind mit groben weißen Holzlatten verkleidet.
Photo: Philippe Saharoff/Inside

102/103 The simple bathroom is lined with white wood. *Salle de bains, sobre lambrissée de bois blanc.* Schlichtes, mit weißem Holz verschaltes Badezimmer.
Les Arnajons, Le Puy Sainte Reparade
Photo: Philippe Saharoff/Inside

104/105 View in the old mirror decorated with large tassels. *Vieux miroir orné de gros glands.* Blick in einen alten Spiegel, der mit dicken Quasten dekoriert ist.
Les Arnajons, Le Puy Sainte Reparade
Photo: Philippe Saharoff/Inside

106/107 Façade of a Provençal farmhouse. *Façade de ferme provençale.* Fassade eines provenzialischen Bauernhauses.
Photo: Guillaume de Laubier/Maison Française
Inside

108/109 Salon with a stone fireplace and a large row of windows to enjoy the view. *Salon avec cheminée de pierre et vastes fenêtres pour jouir de la vue.* Salon mit einem Kamin aus Stein und großer Fensterfront für den Ausblick.
Photo: Deidi von Schaewen

110/111 View of the dining area, which is part of the open living room. *Vue du coin salle à manger, aménagé dans un angle du grand salon.* Ansicht der Essecke, die Teil des offenen Wohnzimmers ist. Architect: Arne Tenglaad
Photo: Deidi von Schaewen

112/113 The salon, decorated Moroccan-style. *Salon aménagé à la marocaine.* Im marokkanischen Stil eingerichteter Salon.
Architect: Arne Tenglaad
Photo: Deidi von Schaewen

114/115 Bedroom with old decorated beds and sunshine yellow walls. *Chambre à coucher avec lits anciens décorés et murs jaune soleil.* Schlafzimmer mit alten verzierten Betten und sonnengelben Wänden.
Photo: Deidi von Schaewen

116/117 Natural stone façade of an old house with evening lighting. *Façade en pierre naturelle et son élcairage nocturne.* Natursteinfassade eines alten Hauses in abendlicher Beleuchtung.
Photo: Mirjam Bleeker/Taverne Agency;
Production: Jet Krings

118/119 A country kitchen with a crockery cupboard, fireplace and wooden table. *Cuisine campagnarde avec buffet, cheminée et table en bois.* Landhausküche mit Geschirrschrank, Kamin und Holztisch.
Photo: Mirjam Bleeker/Taverne Agency;
Production: Jet Krings

120/121 Living room with set of chairs in French Empire style. *Salon avec en-semble de chaises style Empire.* Wohnraum mit Sitzgruppe im französischen Empirestil.
Photo: Mirjam Bleeker/Taverne Agency;
Production: Jet Krings

122/123 View into the bedroom with sky-blue walls. *Vue de la chambre à coucher aux murs bleu ciel.* Blick ins Schlafzimmer mit himmelblauen Wänden.
Photo: Mirjam Bleeker/Taverne Agency;
Production: Jet Krings

124/125 Bathroom with freestanding bathtub. *Salle de bains avec baignoire non encastrée.* Badezimmer mit frei stehender Wanne.
Photo: Mirjam Bleeker/Taverne Agency;
Production: Jet Krings

126/127 This veranda is a dream of a place for sunbathing. *Cette terrasse est l'endroit rêvé pour un bain de soleil.* Die Veranda ist ein traumhafter Platz für ein Bad in der Sonne.
Photo: Mirjam Bleeker/Taverne Agency;
Production: Jet Krings

"... slices of roast kid, mountain cheese, must jam, figs, muscatel grapes. All washed down with that excellent châteauneuf des papes, which glows in the glasses with such a lovely rose colour..."

Alphonse Daudet: The Poet Mistral, in: *Letters from my Windmill*

«...un morceau de chevreau rôti, du fromage de montagne, de la confiture de moût, des figues, des raisins muscats. Le tout arrosé de ce bon châteauneuf des papes qui a une si belle couleur rose dans les verres...»

Alphonse Daudet, Le Poète Mistral, dans *Les Lettres de mon moulin*

»...ein Stück Ziegenlammbraten, Bergkäse, Weinmostkonfitüre, Feigen, Muskattrauben. Das Ganze begossen mit dem köstlichen Châteauneuf des Papes, der in den Gläsern eine so schöne rosige Farbe hat...«

Alphonse Daudet, Der Dichter Mistral, in: *Briefe aus meiner Windmühle*

DETAILS

Détails   Details

134 A road lined with cypresses and lavender. *Un chemin bordé de cyprès et de lavande.* Eine von Zypressen und Lavendel gesäumte Allee.
Photo: Guy Hervais

136 Zucchini roasted according to a French recipe. *Courgettes grillées à la française.* Geröstete Zucchini, nach französischem Rezept zubereitet.
Photo: Guy Hervais

137 Fresh sage leaves with flowers. *Feuilles de sauge fraîche avec d'une fleur.* Frische Salbeiblätter und Blüte.
Photo: Guy Hervais

138 A place to play boules in the shade. *Terrain de boules à l'ombre.* Im Schatten gelegener Bouleplatz.
Photo: Guy Hervais

140 Refreshing and delicious aperitif. *Un apéritif, aussi délicieux que rafraîchissant.* Erfrischender und köstlicher Aperitif.
Photo: Guy Hervais

141 Marinated tomatoes decorated with rosemary. *Tomates marinées parfumées au romarin.* Marinierte Tomaten,mit Rosmarin angerichtet.
Photo: Guy Hervais

142 View of the old Vaison-la-Romaine. *Vue sur la vieille ville de Vaison-la-Romaine.* Blick auf das alte Vaison-la-Romaine.
Photo: Guy Hervais

144 An old cuddly toy lamb guarding the bed. *Agneau en peluche montant la garde sur un lit.* Ein auf dem Bett wachendes altes Stofflamm.
Photo: Guy Hervais

145 Classic French novel "La Femme" with fresh figs. *Roman classique français «La Femme», avec figues fraîches.* Klassischer französischer Roman »La Femme« und frische Feigen.
Photo: Guy Hervais

146 Laid table with Provençal tablecloth. *Table dressée avec nappe provençale.* Gedeckter Tisch mit provenzialischer Tischdecke.
Photo: Guillaume de Laubier/Maison Française/Inside

148 18th century-woman's bust. *Un buste de femme du 18ᵉ siècle.* Frauenbüste aus dem 18. Jh.
Photo: Guy Hervais

149 Antique wall candleholder on an artistically decorated red wall. *Chandelier mural anciesur mur rouge, décoré avec art.* Antiker Wandkerzenleuchter auf einer künstlerisch gestalteten roten Wand.
Photo: Guy Hervais

150 Autumnally coloured Provençal landscape. *Paysage provençal aux couleurs de l'automne.* Herbstlich gefärbte Landschaft der Provence.
Photo: Guy Hervais

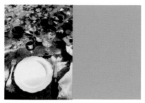

152 Invitingly laid place with beautiful crockery, cutlery and wineglasses. *Très beau couvert, invitant à se mettre à table.* Einladend gedeckter Platz mit wunderschönem Service. Photo: Guy Hervais

154 View into the large dining hall of the Hotel LaMirande, Avignon. *Vue sur la grande salle à manger de l'hôtel La Mirande, Avignon.* Blick in den großen Speisesaal des Hotels La Mirande, Avignon. Photo: Guy Hervais

156/157 Dining hall in the former cardinal's palace. *Salle à manger dans l'ancien palais des cardinaux.* Speisesaal im ehemaligen Kardinalspalast. La Mirande, Avignon Photo: Guy Hervais

159 Old clay pot surrounded by nature in mist. *Ancienne jarre en terre, cuite dans un paysage brumeux.* Altes Tongefäß, umgeben von der im Dunst liegenden Natur. Photo: Guy Hervais

160/161 Sweet-smelling lime-blossom twigs in a vase between two old chairs provides a decorative touch. *Branches parfumées de tilleul en fleur, dans un vase, entre deux sièges anciens.*

Duftende Lindenblütenzweige, in der Vase dekoriert, zwischen zwei alten Sitzmöbeln. Photo: Mirjam Bleeker/Taverne Agency; Production: Jet Krings

162 Towel-holder in a shady bathroom. *Porte-serviettes à l'ombre des aux persiennes.* Handtuchhalter in einem schattigen Badezimmer. Photo: Guillaume de Laubier/Maison Française Inside

164 A small alcove with fragments of old stonepieces. *Niche avec fragments de vieilles pierres travaillées.* Eine kleine Nische mit Bruchstücken alter Werksteine. Photo: Deidi von Schaewen/Philipp Seuilliet

165 Stray cat. *Chat en promenade.* Streunende Katze. Photo: Deidi von Schaewen/Philippe Seuilliet

166 Cat on a window-sill. *Chat sur le rebord d'une fenêtre.* Katze auf einer Fensterbank. Photo: Philippe Saharoff/Inside

168 Traditionally furnished bedroom in the hotel La Mirande. *Chambre à coucher de style traditionnel à l'hôtel de La Mirande.* Traditionell eingerichtetes Schlafzimmer im Hotel La Mirande. Photo: Guy Hervais

169 Breakfast with home-made jam. *Petit-déjeuner avec confiture maison.* Petit-déjeuner mit hausgemachter Marmelade. La Mirande, Avignon Photo: Guy Hervais

170 Antique taps with an old pharmacist's jar. *Robinets anciens avec vieux pot d'apothicaire.* Antike Armaturen mit einem alten Apothekengefäß. Photo: Maison Française/Françoise Lemarchand/Inside

172 Four-poster bed with turquoise and white striped wall. *Lit à baldaquin sur murs rayées blanc/turquoise.* Himmelbett vor türkis und weiß gestrichener Wand. Photo: Philippe Saharoff/Inside

175 Ironing board with old iron. *Planches à repasser avec fers anciens.* Bügelbrett mit alten Bügeleisen. Photo: Philippe Saharoff/Inside

176 View of the landscape through the open window. *Vue sur le paysage par la fênetre ouverte.* Ausblick durch das geöffnete Fenster auf die Landschaft. Photo: Mirjam Bleeker/Taverne Agency; Production: Jet Krings

178/179 Basket filled with fresh herbs. *Panier rempli de fines herbes.* Korb, gefüllt mit frischen Kräutern. Photo: Maison Française/Françoise Lemarchand/Inside

180 Bathroom done in blue and white. *Salle de bains à carreaux bleus et blancs.* In blau und weiß gehaltenes Badezimmer. Photo: Maison Française/Françoise Lemarchand/Inside

182 Old bed with wrought iron trimmings and white linen bedding. *Lit ancien en fer forgé. Draps et taies de lin blanc.* Verschnörkeltes altes, mit weißer Leinenbettwäsche bezogenes Bett. Photo: Maison Française/Françoise Lemarchand/Inside

183 White wooden cupboard with a basket full of olive twigs. *Armoire de bois blanc avec corbeille remplie de branches d'olivier.* Weißer Holzschrank mit einem Korb voller Olivenzweige. Photo: Maison Française/Françoise Lemarchand/Inside

184 Beautiful seating area in Mediterranean style. *Joli coin repos, de style méditerranéen.* Traumhafte Sitzecke, im mediterranen Stil gehalten. Photo: Mirjam Bleeker/Taverne Agency; Production: Jet Krings

186/187 Cheese board with fresh local produce. *Plateau de fromage avec produits de la région.* Käseplatte mit frischen Produkten aus der Region. Photo: Mirjam Bleeker/Taverne Agency Production: Jet Krings

190

ADDRESSES / ADRESSES / ADRESSEN

La Mirande
4, Place de la Mirande
84000 Avignon
France
Tel: +33 (0) 490 859 393
Fax: +33 (0) 490 862 685
mirande@la-mirande.fr
www.la-mirande.fr

La Bastide de Marie
Route de Bonnieux
Quartier de la Verrerie
84560 Ménerbes
France
Tel: + 33 (0) 490 723 020
Fax: +33 (0) 490 725 420
bastidemarie@c-h-m.com
www.c-h-m.com

Provence Interiors
Lisa Lovatt-Smith
Hardcover, 300 pp.

Gardens of Provence
Marie-Françoise Valéry
Padded cover, 176 pp.

"These seductive little books have slick production values, excellent illustrations, and smart texts. Each one is a fast-food, high-energy fix on the topic at hand."
—*The New York Times Book Review*, New York, on the ICON series

"Buy them all and add some pleasure to your life."

All-American Ads 40ˢ
Ed. Jim Heimann

All-American Ads 50ˢ
Ed. Jim Heimann

Angels
Gilles Néret

Architecture Now!
Ed. Philip Jodidio

Art Now
Eds. Burkhard Riemschneider,
Uta Grosenick

Atget's Paris
Ed. Hans Christian Adam

Best of Bizarre
Ed. Eric Kroll

Bizarro Postcards
Ed. Jim Heimann

Karl Blossfeldt
Ed. Hans Christian Adam

California, Here I Come
Ed. Jim Heimann

50ˢ Cars
Ed. Jim Heimann

Chairs
Charlotte & Peter Fiell

Classic Rock Covers
Michael Ochs

Description of Egypt
Ed. Gilles Néret

Design of the 20ᵗʰ Century
Charlotte & Peter Fiell

Designing the 21ˢᵗ Century
Charlotte & Peter Fiell

Dessous
Lingerie as Erotic Weapon
Gilles Néret

Devils
Gilles Néret

Digital Beauties
Ed. Julius Wiedemann

Robert Doisneau
Ed. Jean-Claude Gautrand

Eccentric Style
Ed. Angelika Taschen

Encyclopaedia Anatomica
Museo La Specola, Florence

Erotica 17ᵗʰ–18ᵗʰ Century
From Rembrandt to Fragonard
Gilles Néret

Erotica 19ᵗʰ Century
From Courbet to Gauguin
Gilles Néret

Erotica 20ᵗʰ Century, Vol. I
From Rodin to Picasso
Gilles Néret

Erotica 20ᵗʰ Century, Vol. II
From Dalí to Crumb
Gilles Néret

Future Perfect
Ed. Jim Heimann

The Garden at Eichstätt
Basilius Besler

HR Giger
HR Giger

Indian Style
Ed. Angelika Taschen

Kitchen Kitsch
Ed. Jim Heimann

Krazy Kids' Food
Eds. Steve Roden,
Dan Goodsell

London Style
Ed. Angelika Taschen

Male Nudes
David Leddick

Man Ray
Ed. Manfred Heiting

Mexicana
Ed. Jim Heimann

Native Americans
Edward S. Curtis
Ed. Hans Christian Adam

New York Style
Ed. Angelika Taschen

**Extra/Ordinary Objects,
Vol. I**
Ed. Colors Magazine

15ᵗʰ Century Paintings
Rose-Marie and Rainer Hagen

16ᵗʰ Century Paintings
Rose-Marie and Rainer Hagen

Paris-Hollywood
Serge Jacques
Ed. Gilles Néret

Penguin
Frans Lanting

Photo Icons, Vol. I
Hans-Michael Koetzle

Photo Icons, Vol. II
Hans-Michael Koetzle

20ᵗʰ Century Photography
Museum Ludwig Cologne

Pin-Ups
Ed. Burkhard Riemschneider

Giovanni Battista Piranesi
Luigi Ficacci

Provence Style
Ed. Angelika Taschen

Pussy-Cats
Gilles Néret

Redouté's Roses
Pierre-Joseph Redouté

Robots and Spaceships
Ed. Teruhisa Kitahara

Seaside Style
Ed. Angelika Taschen

Seba: Natural Curiosities
I. Müsch, R. Willmann, J. Rust

See the World
Ed. Jim Heimann

Eric Stanton
Reunion in Ropes & Other
Stories
Ed. Burkhard Riemschneider

Eric Stanton
She Dominates All & Other
Stories
Ed. Burkhard Riemschneider

Tattoos
Ed. Henk Schiffmacher

Edward Weston
Ed. Manfred Heiting

ICONS